Book Description

Does your child lie out of impulse without any reason? Do they hide stuff from you and keep secrets? Does it make it hard for you to trust them when they are telling the truth? Do you feel betrayed every time your child chooses to keep their private life secret? Are you stalking them on social media to know what is going on in their life and head?

These are all signs of a lack of transparency in parent-child relationships. But you aren't alone in this. Many parents raising adolescents and teenagers complain about the change in behavior and an increase in the number of lies told.

As parents, it is really hard for us to distinguish between the truth and the lies. However, if we teach our children good values and morals from the beginning, most of the lies can be prevented. In *How Parents Can Teach Children to Live with Transparency*, we help parents learn about the many ways they can help their kids adopt behaviors and habits that promote honesty and openness. We teach them how they can become their child's friends when they need it. We also look at the many mistakes parents unknowingly make when teaching their kids about the importance of honesty and candidness.

Here's all that you can expect to learn from this book:

- Understanding honesty and its role
- Why kids lie
- The nature of lies they tell and the type of liar they are
- The difference between secrecy and privacy
- Things children hide from their parents
- What are safe and unsafe secrets and how to respond to them
- How healthy communication between parents and children can foster honesty
- How parents can be role models for their kids to preach about honesty

Written in a simple, easy-to-read and engaging manner, this book is the perfect guide to help you identify the mistakes you make when trying to raise an honest child and how to spot them early on and raise them better.

How Parents Can Teach Children to Live With Transparency

A Whole Heart Approach to Effectively Raising Honest and Candid Kids Without Secrets

Frank Dixon

professional advice. The content within this book has been derived from various sources. Please consult a licensed professional before attempting any techniques outlined in this book.

By reading this document, the reader agrees that under no circumstances is the author responsible for any losses, direct or indirect, that are incurred as a result of the use of the information contained within this document, including, but not limited to, errors, omissions, or inaccuracies.

Before we begin, I have something special waiting for you. An action-packed 1 page printout with a few quick & easy tips taken from this book that you can start using today to become a better parent right now!

It's my gift to you, free of cost. Think of it as my way of saying thank you to you for purchasing this book.

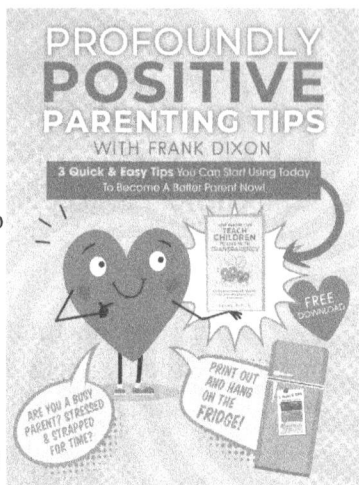

Claim your download of Profoundly Positive Parenting with Frank Dixon by scanning the QR code below and join my mailing list.

Sign up below to grab your free copy, print it out and hang it on the fridge!

Sign Up By Scanning The QR Code With Your Phone's Camera To Be Redirected To A Page To Enter Your Email And Receive INSTANT Access To Your Download

Before we jump in, I'd like to express my gratitude. I know this mustn't be the first book you came across and yet you still decided to give it a read. There are numerous courses and guides you could have picked instead that promise to make you an ideal and well-rounded parent while raising your children to be the best they can be.

But for some reason, mine stood out from the rest and this makes me the happiest person on the planet right now. If you stick with it, I promise this will be a worthwhile read.

In the pages that follow, you're going to learn the best parenting skills so that your child can grow to become the best version of themselves and in doing so experience a meaningful understanding of what it means to be an effective parent.

Notable Quotes About Parenting

"Children Must Be Taught How To Think, Not What To Think."

— Margaret Mead

"It's easier to build strong children than to fix broken men [or women]."

- Frederick Douglass

"Truly great friends are hard to find, difficult to leave, and impossible to forget."

— George Randolf

"Nothing in life is to be feared, it is only to be understood. Now is the time to understand more, so that we may fear less."

— Scientist Marie Curie

Table of Contents

Introduction

A decade ago, raising sensible, good, and practical kids was rather straightforward. But not today, at least not in this age of rapid connectivity and the internet. With nearly everyone having a Wi-Fi router in their homes and 4G data packages on phones, the way we raise kids and talk to them about healthy values has changed. But this exposure has also opened new opportunities for parents to learn and reach out to expert advice and seek professional help when facing problems with their kids' upbringing. Kids, too, have started to be more inquisitive than before. But being a double-edged sword, we still need to figure out if the pros outweigh the cons when it comes to increased internet access. The dark side, of course, includes easy access to obscenity and trigger-causing information which can lead to gadget addiction.

To say the least, the role of the parents is to be ever vigilant and keep a keen eye on what the child is viewing and taking in before they are drawn to some dark cesspool. Why?

Because children begin to lie and hide things. They lie about where they were, who they were with, what they were doing, and what they plan to do next. They keep secrets and do things that their parents would otherwise tell them not to. This lack of transparency in the parent-child relationship can turn into a lifelong habit and make things uncomfortable between the two of you. You want them to open up with you, share their thoughts and ideas, not fear coming to you when they want to confess something.

Children must be taught about the repercussions their sneaking and dishonesty can have in order to discourage the forming of these habits.

Honest and open conversations about anything and everything is the way to tackle this. Having worked with families who wished they had spent more time with their kids getting to know them better, it is easy to look at the prevalent problem. Parents in their old age regret not having a household that encouraged open dialogues because their children left the nest the minute they turned 16. With more than 76 million American baby boomers looking to retire, it is time we start having this conversation and talking about the importance of good and healthy family structures and what they look like.

If you still resist the idea, you must be ready for the consequences. Little to no openness can lead to misunderstandings between the child and the parents, where the parent feels insignificant and the child feels that the parent doesn't care enough. Parenting has to be a partnership where families thrive by coming closer, addressing critical issues, and making decisions that benefit everyone equally.

It all starts with being honest and transparent. This is what the general idea of the book is about. We want parents to teach their kids to be more open and honest. We want to help them understand why children sometimes lie. We also want to pinpoint the grave mistakes they make intentionally or unintentionally which lead to children lying and being secretive.

So, without further ado, let's kick this off with the first aspect of transparency: honesty and integrity.

Chapter 1: Being Honest – Is It Important?

What does being transparent really mean? Does it mean telling the whole world about all that you do or don't do? Does it mean being honest at all times, even when it hurts to hear the truth? Does it mean having no secrets to keep or share with someone?

We believe it means trying our best not to lie about or hide information and actions that prevent the forming of a healthy relationship. We are already living in a world where nothing holds more importance than honest relationships, but even when living under the same roof, we still struggle with winning someone's trust. Ask yourself this: as a parent, do you trust that your child can do no wrong? Maybe you like to think so, but can you be certain about all their actions and behaviors behind closed doors or when you aren't with them? Can you vouch for them being honest with you 100% of the time? Can you say the same for yourself? Are you being honest when you make up lies to skip brunch with your friends or lie to your wife about getting drinks with your office colleagues?

There is nothing to be ashamed of as it is in our nature to lie, but that certainly doesn't mean you allow yourself or your kids to get away with it. As humans, we are afraid of being mistreated, misjudged, or rejected. So we trick ourselves into lying and getting away with things. We wear a mask to please everyone. We hide who we really are. So do our kids!

But what if we were to tell you that being transparent was the way out of all this?

Being transparent allows us to stay stress-free. When you are open with someone, there is little worry in your mind. When you have clear intentions about something and are willing to expose yourself and your feelings, you allow others to see the real you. There are less unpleasant surprises when we are honest and things go well for everyone. When you are transparent, you can't be manipulated. Your intentions become straightforward and there is little secrecy involved.

Despite these benefits, you will be shocked to know that we, including the kids, lie on average one to six times per day. And if we are having a conversation of approximately ten minutes, we are sure to lie at least two times during it (Feldman, 2002).

But do we really need to deceive or tell half-truths as often as we do?

According to a research study from the University of Chicago, people are much better at handling the truth than we think or credit them for (Levine & Cohen, 2018). Initially, they may act surprised or even hurt, but it is less hurt that is experienced when they find out the truth later. We do the same with our kids. To keep them safe or out of harm's way, we lie to them instead of having open conversations. We assume they won't take the truth well or be bad at taking critical feedback, but that isn't always the truth. In the research, the authors asked respondents to be completely honest with a close relation and monitored their reactions. Keep in mind, the conversations were anything but comfortable and involved several sensitive and personal questions. Many questions resulted in negative feedback, but the findings revealed that the receiver seemed okay with the truth.

Keeping this in mind, it is safe to suggest that speaking the truth and not hiding or manipulating it is the best policy.

Honesty and Wellbeing

Presented at the American Psychological Association's 120th annual convention, this brief study led by Anita E. Kelly, a psychology professor at the University of Notre Dame suggested that on average, Americans tell approximately 11 lies per week (Kelly, 2012). She, along with her fellow researchers wanted to study if telling fewer lies resulted in improved health or not.

The study consisted of about 110 people, 34% adults and 66% college students. Their ages ranged from 18 to 71. The participants were divided into two groups: one of them was asked to make an effort to stop lying for the next ten weeks, while the others weren't. Each week, both groups were called in for a polygraph test to determine how many lies they told during the week. Some tests related to their health and wellbeing were also conducted. Participants in the no-lie group reported that what caused them to stop lying over the weeks was the avoidance of fake excuses and exaggerations. They told the researchers that whenever they felt like lying as a response to some questions asked by someone, they resorted to asking a different question in return. After studying their test results and comparing them with the results of the second group, researchers were able to notice a significant change in their health comparisons. The first group seemed to have improved their health throughout the 10-weeks experiment. This was evident by looking at their stress levels, which showed a major decline. They also reported fewer headaches and sore throats.

This study provides enough evidence to believe that being truthful, honest, and transparent is what helps keep our health in check. It prevents us from feeling stressed, anxious, or nervous – responses that are triggered when we tell a lie.

Honesty Reduces Stress

In the magazine Shape, Dr. Arthur Markman reports that every time we tell a lie, our nervous system releases the stress hormone cortisol into our brain (Heid, n.d.). Cortisol sets in motion our immune system, which starts fighting against this imbalance in the brain. The more lies we tell to keep up with the first one, the more cortisol is released. Anxiety takes over and we become stressed. If left untreated, this can lead to other medical and emotional issues like irritation, and anger. Since we don't want to get caught, we keep adding onto the first lie to save ourselves from embarrassment, without realizing the harmful effects lying has on our brain, body, and mood.

Those who often find themselves lying to get away with something or cover up for a mistake also report anxiety in the form of a worn-out immune system, headaches, heart palpitations, insomnia, and dizziness. It is easy enough to recognize the reasons behind why many middle-aged people face heart-related issues today. The added pressure of work, increasing competition, and high expectations that compels one to lie. But our kids don't need that, and we can prevent this from becoming their future reality by teaching them the right values and ethics, which includes being transparent.

Honesty and Future Success

It doesn't matter if our kids have just started to walk or asked for a car as their graduation present, we want them to have the best of everything. We want them to be better than who we were as kids and do better than we ever did. We want them to succeed, follow their passions, and live life as freely as they can.

What if we told you that all of this is possible if you just teach them good values and high morals?

Being honest and transparent cuts through the red tape, it minimizes frustrations and distractions, and it eliminates indecisiveness. When we are honest with ourselves and others, we move faster towards our goals because our intent and conscience are clear. We live the way we feel. There is little to no disguise when it comes to speaking about our plans and working towards them. We don't expect our children to know what they really want from the minute they step into this world, but clarity will help them make the right decisions, beneficial to them.

Honest actions and speech gain the attention of others and that goes for professionals too. No manager or employer would want to hire a dishonest employee that hides behind lies to conceal their mistakes. They also wouldn't want to hire someone who has a bad reputation. Everyone, including employers, want to be influenced by someone that holds honesty and transparency important. It is no secret that good ethics and moral conduct are the fundamental components of professional success. Being honest is more than just following all the rules and regulations. It is about having values and principles that make you an example for others

Think about this: if you raise a child who is dishonest and lacks integrity, no one would like to be their friend. When they eventually step into the professional field, none of their colleagues will trust them; no one will appreciate an employee that lies, claims credit for the work of others, steals office supplies, and makes up a lie to prove themselves innocent after getting caught. Right now, these may not seem like BIG things to you but let us remind you that these seemingly insignificant things add up over time and can ruin a reputation.

This is why you have to start today. Not only will being honest and transparent save your little one embarrassment and shame, but it will also improve their long term prospects and wellbeing.

Chapter 2: Lies, Lies, and More Lies...

Ever wondered how easy it would be to spot a lie if our noses started to grow like Pinocchio's? We would notice the second our kids lied to us. But then, it would also be harder to parent them as we lie to them too. Yes, the cookie jar wasn't stolen by thieves and their favorite blanket isn't in the wash.

In this chapter, we explore the world of lying in detail. We will discuss the many different types of lies and liars, and we will debate whether lying can EVER be a good thing and in what conditions it is considered acceptable, if at all.

But first, what does lying mean? According to the dictionary, lying refers to making a false statement. However, that is not enough for us to work with. The reason we can't simply define what qualifies as a lie and what doesn't is because there is an issue involving intent and expectation. For starters, no one just casually lies. No one casually offers a misleading answer to a question. There has to be some form of motivation involved.

To grasp the concept of lying better, we need to take a look at the types of liars as well as the types of lies kids in particular resort to, to determine if all lying is bad or if it can be good – if the intention is justifiable.

The Many Faces of Liars

As believed, liars can be of different types. Children usually don't know the difference between the depths of the lie they are telling but as a parent, you must know.

- White Liars: liars who have a habit of hiding things or telling half-truth are white liars. They lie because they assume they are protecting someone from harm. This involves a child telling you that the food you cooked for them is delicious because they want a favor from you. This type of lying is more akin to sugar-coating, so it can be let go if it occurs occasionally.

- Occasional Liars: as the name suggests, kids who lie infrequently are occasional liars. Occasional liars actually have the habit of eventually confessing to their lies or the wrong they did which resulted in them telling a lie. They are quick to seek forgiveness and show a willingness to work on themselves to prevent it from happening again. They confess because they are overcome by guilt and can't keep quiet.

- Careless Liars: liars who don't care about how many times they have lied or about the severity and consequences of their lies. They are masters of twisted stories and thus aren't very reliable. For example, it is that kid in class who brags about going on luxury yacht trips every summer when in reality they just spend it visiting grandma. They never confess to their lies even when confronted and will tell more to cover up the previous ones.

- Compulsive Liars: these are the worst kind of liars, who lie out of habit. Every word out of their mouth is inconsistent and they prefer lying over telling the truth. Since habits are formed after repeated action or behavior, many people believe that adult compulsive liars may have had traumatic or problematic childhoods, where lying may have been a necessity.

Types of Lies Most Children Concoct

Now that we have identified the types of liars, we can move on to looking at the types of lies told most commonly by kids and teenagers.

We have *imaginary lies* where the child, due to poor comprehension about what is real and what isn't, exaggerated a scenario to seek attention. For instance, your child talking about how their toys move at night after everyone goes to bed.

Then come *need-based lies*, which are most common with kids aged between three to five. Need-based lies involve emotional manipulation so that the children can get something they want. For example, a child complaining about pain in their arm to avoid doing their chores in the house.

Thirdly, we have *social lies*, often spoken when someone doesn't want to engage socially. It is a child asking to skip school because their tummy hurts on the day of a big test or presentation.

There are also *routine lies*, where the child just can't control themselves from telling a lie. Routine lying can develop into *pathological lying*, which can point to a personality disorder and thus should be discussed with a child specialist or therapist.

Fear-based lies are lies spoken out of fear or danger of being caught or punished. These are mostly spoken when the child has done something they know to be wrong and wants to cover it up. They don't want to be punished and resort to telling a lie.

And finally, we have *admirable lies* where children exaggerate about their qualifications, skills, or successes to impress others. An example of this would be a child joining a new school and telling everybody about his extra-curricular skills in an exaggerated manner.

Can Lying be a Good Thing?

As parents, we want our kids to never lie. We think that honesty is a moral imperative and we are keen on instilling it as a belief in our children. Besides, we have all read *The Boy Who Cried Wolf* and

Pinocchio. We see kids who lie as primed for trouble in the future. But what if we told you that they were smarter and more vigilant?

According to some scientists, lying among children is a sign of intelligence. We already know that kids learn to lie by the time they turn two. They have been lying before then too, but once they turn two, they start to lie because they see lying as a means of getting what they want.

In an experiment conducted in the mid-1980s, a team of researchers led by developmental psychologist Michael Lewis set out to find out how easily kids lie and how easy it is for adults to recognize the lie. They would ask a child in a room to NOT peek at the toy hidden behind them in the room; the researcher would then leave the room after making an excuse. Approximately 80% of the children looked at the toy within seconds of the researcher leaving the room. When the researcher returned and asked the kids if they had taken a peek, many of them lied about it. What the kids didn't know was that they were being recorded throughout the experiment. When they lied, their response and expressions were recorded too. The footage of the second half of the experiment was shown to social workers, police officers, primary school teachers, and even judges, who were asked to spot the liars but couldn't. Finally, the parents of the kids were called upon but even they were unable to detect the lie.

The kids who had lied about not peeking at the toy showed a higher verbal IQ than those who didn't lie, and the kids who didn't peek at the toy at all had the highest IQ.

As interesting as this is, it doesn't mean that lying should be celebrated. It is still a negative habit and your child should keep at a distance from it. Lying should only be acceptable when it is aimed to spare someone from hurt, fear, or trouble. Meaning, you can't make your child tell that truth about the meatloaf Aunt Julie served at Christmas. Imagine your kid telling her that it was so bad that even your dog refused to eat it. Would that be okay?

Besides, we have been lying to our kids for years. If they still believe in an old guy bringing them presents once a year, you have been lying to them. Even you know why you do it and why it is considered acceptable.

Make it a point to teach your children what kind of lying is acceptable, when the lie is to prevent hurt or fear in others, especially those we care about like our family and friends.

Chapter 3: Preventing the Habit of Lying

Now that we understand the basics of lying and the different types of lies and liars, the next important step is the identification of whether you are raising a child who is a liar or not. Again, keep in mind that this section isn't to demean or judge your capacity as a parent: there's just a problem that needs to be addressed and some work to counter it.

Although it can be almost impossible to detect a good lie, there are still some signs useful for spotting a liar, especially a child or a teenager, who is still learning to lie. It may take you some practice to notice these in the beginning but the more you notice, the clearer they will become. Once you have spotted a lie, no need to yell at the child. There are various ways to handle it, which we will discuss later in this chapter.

Signs I am Raising a Liar

Here's what you need to look out for when trying to catch a lying child.

- They take long pauses before answering: this suggests there is some thinking going on which involves concocting a story to tell. When they are speaking the truth, they already know all the facts and don't need to think or pause before answering. Pauses indicate they are hiding something.

- They change the subject or try to keep their sentences short. When asked a question, they will either try to avoid it completely by going off-topic or tell only a fraction of the truth. For instance, if you asked them if they went to the library after school, they might respond with something like, "Hey do you know there was a guest at school today?" Notice how they haven't really answered the question and just stated a loosely connected fact.
- Their pitch changes. When someone tries to lie, a difference in their vocal pitch can be observed. Their answers will seem hasty, loud, or uttered with a stutter. It is most common with occasional liars as they start to feel guilty.
- They talk faster. Remember the first sign? It suggested that when someone lies, they usually take long pauses between questions. But lack of silence or speaking faster than normal is also a sign of lying. When kids and teenagers begin to talk quickly when they normally don't communicate in that manner, it can also be a sign that they are trying hard to convince you of something.
- Their eye movement changes: liars mostly avoid eye contact. This is also a sign to look for if they are consistently avoiding looking you in the eyes and are looking down.

Why Do Kids Lie?

Lying is rather common among adolescents and teenagers. According to one study, 96% of kids lie at home at one point or another. The study also classified the number of lies based on the ages of the children. For instance, it was found that kids aged four and five lie every two hours, whereas kids aged six and older lie every hour on average. If this is true, they are lying to us at least five to six times per day, which is shocking.

No one wants their kids to be liars. However, this isn't the real worry we are going to address here. The real worry is this: why do kids lie? What motivates them to resort to dishonesty? Why do they hide the truth? Researchers believe one or more of these reasons are to blame.

They may not know they are lying as they are too young to distinguish between reality and imagination. They are simply making up tales to make routine tasks seem interesting.

Secondly, it seems like a new thing they have just been introduced to and are testing out the behavior. They have seen it work and are excited to be using it often. Maybe it has kept them safe from punishment or impressed their parents, so they see it as a rewarding behavior.

Another reason is to make themselves seem impressive, talented, or to inflate their self-esteem.

This is most common among kids suffering from a lack of confidence. They exaggerate and tell lies. They lie to gain the approval of others and to boost their self-esteem when they get away with it. Lies make them appear smarter and special in the eyes of others – something that they love and crave.

A child may also lie to avoid getting in trouble or avoid doing something unpleasant. When this is the case, it is important to note the trigger and focus on that instead of lecturing the child about the danger of lying.

Another reason to lie is out of fear or when kids want to take the focus off themselves. For example, if a kid is shy and doesn't like to attend big gatherings, they may make up excuses to skip them and stay at home instead.

Kids who want to be accepted by their parents, peers, and friends also lie sometimes. According to one study, when kids feel that they won't be able to live up to the standards and expectations set by their parents, they lie about reaching them to avoid punishment and shame (Smith & Rizzo, 2017). They know if they tell the truth, they will be held accountable for falling short, but if they lie, they might avoid getting in trouble. During the research, kids aged four to nine were given two stories to read. Each story had the main character doing something bad and lying about it. In the first story, the main character stole candy from a buddy, and in the second, they pushed another kid from a swing. Half the kids read the stories where the candy-stealer confessed about their wrongdoing to their mothers and the swing-pusher lied. The other half read the stories where the candy-stealer lied and the swing-pusher confessed to the crime.

Throughout the reading session, the researchers kept asking the kids what they thought of the main character and of their crime.

At the same time, the researchers also called in the parents of those children and presented them with a questionnaire asking them to rate their child's lying behavior. The questionnaire included questions such as: "Do they confess to a crime?", "Do they seem impatient or out of character when lying?" etc.

The children whose parents rated them better at telling the truth were also the same that suggested that the main character would feel much better if they came clean with their parents about their crime. These findings suggest that children are honest when they think it pleases their parents.

The Dangers of Lying

When kids develop a taste for lying because their lying saved them from their parents, they form a pattern. This is highly dangerous as it is hard to get rid of a bad habit, especially when the kid is growing up and argues about everything. They present you with all the excuses in the world as to why they lied in the first place without being sorry or ashamed. This breaks the trust in the relationship as it becomes harder for you to believe them, even when they aren't lying.

So, when you are trying to sit them down and talk to them about it, don't forget about the dangers mentioned below.

It Isn't Good for Their Health

We already know how lying adds to stress in the body which can lead to anxiety. As a parent, you want to do anything you can to prevent your children from developing any health issues.

Things Will Only Get More Complicated

It would be much easier if we lied about something just once and everyone forgot about it, but a lie always comes back to bite us. And then, we have to tell more lies and then more lies to cover up for the second batch of lies. The cycle never stops – unless we come clean about it.

You Lose All Trust in the Eyes of Others

An honest person is respected by everyone. A dishonest person isn't. People stop trusting you or your word. Your value declines in their eyes and no matter what you do, they will always see a liar in you and avoid being close to you or rely on you for anything. If this isn't punishment enough, we don't know what is.

It Is a Lot of Work

No one ever said that lying was supposed to be the easy way out. True, it might have kept your child out of trouble once or twice, but it needs a lot of work. There is so much to remember and it can be hard to recall as isn't natural. Imagine if you told your boss that you were sick and thus didn't show up to work once and then when asked about it again the next month, you failed to remember and make up another lie instead? What are the chances you will get away with it? What if you get caught? Are you willing to lose your self-respect for something as little as this? Let your child know that another danger of lying is that you have to keep up with the same story. If there are any inconsistencies, their chances of being caught increase.

Others Feel Devalued

When you are caught lying to someone, it is telling them that you don't value them enough to come clean. Where does that leave the relationship, be it between a parent and a child, a child and their friends, or a child and their peers and teachers?

Lying Can Turn Into a Bad Habit Hard to Get Rid Of

Once the child starts to lie, it can be really hard to stop. It is like an addiction: the more you lie and get away with them, the more power it gives you. If you develop a taste for it, you will eventually turn into a pathological liar that lies about everything without a reason or cause. According to one study, the more we lie, the easier it becomes, and the more frequently we speak the truth, the harder lying becomes (Verschuere, Spruyt, Meijer, & Otgaar, 2010).

There Is Little Sense of Accomplishment

When we lie, we deprive ourselves of feelings of accomplishment, even if our lie succeeds. Triumph originating from a lie is short-lived and filled with self-contempt and guilt. The victory seems hollow and does little to boost our self-esteem in the long run. It even undermines our self-image.

And Finally, Lies Can Mislead

If you have told someone a lie, an image of the event or story you concocted sets in their mind. They start believing it to be the truth and get misled. For instance, if a child tells their parents that they have finished their homework, they might plan a night out for fun. But when they find out that the child lied, it will break their heart.

Chapter 4: Ssshh, Don't Tell My Parents!

All kids hide the truth or keep secrets. Even when they are honest most of the time, there are still things that they like to keep from their parents. As they grow up, they figure out what behaviors get them reward and praises, and what gets them in trouble. Since the temptation of the things that end up in arguments or punishments is bigger, they continue to attempt them without letting anyone know.

In this chapter, we discuss the many reasons why kids, especially teenagers, lie to their parents and keep secrets. But first, let's make one thing clear – are secrecy and privacy the same? Or are they the two sides of the same coin?

Secrecy Isn't Privacy

In the words of Dr. Laura Schlessinger, privacy means withholding information that isn't of concern to someone. Its disclosure won't impact others and keeping it to yourself won't affect or harm a parent or partner. Secrecy, on the other hand, is withholding information that directly affects the wellbeing of a parent or partner and can have a detrimental effect. Thus, privacy is acceptable, and secrecy isn't.

To understand it in simpler terms, privacy involves inobservance. For example, you take a bath. This is something you can keep private. It is something that concerns no one but you. The same applies to our dreams and fantasies. They are ours to share or not share with someone because it won't make a big difference in their lives. It is solely on you to decide when to share or if, to share it with someone. For example, you can choose to keep your passion for playing the piano from your child. You can spend your whole life keeping that secret, or you can decide to share it with them.

Secrecy involves hiding. It isn't the same as privacy and it stems from a deliberate effort to keep something in the dark. Secrecy has the potential to negatively impact the lives of others. When such secrets are revealed, they can create feelings of insecurity, betrayal, and hurt. An example of this would be you hiding from your kids that they were adopted or that they have other siblings.

Why Do Kids Prefer Secrecy?

In a PBS Frontline Special in 1999 titled *The Lost Children of Rockdale County*, the narrators told a story about a syphilis outbreak in a wealthy suburb in Atlanta. After evaluating the cases, the health officials reported that the majority of the affected were teenagers, some as young as thirteen years old. Further investigation revealed that some teenagers had more than one sexual partner, with some having dozens and being engaged in all sorts of risky sexual activities. Even more shocking was that these kids didn't come from broken families and neither were they abused or homeless. Most of them were from typical families. The parents were completely unaware of their kids being involved in sexual activities at all.

The reason this story is important here is that most of the teens suffering from syphilis knew that there was something wrong with them but kept it a secret. This suggests that kids, especially teens have a world of their own that excludes anyone that isn't their age or a friend. Their secret lives are the result of a longing to be a part of a cult and do things that make them seem cool – things that their parents would never approve of.

Other than that, kids also hide things out of shame and guilt, especially when they have been hurt in one form or the other. For example, they will hide sexual assault or bullying from their parents or elder siblings because they feel they are somehow to blame for what happened to them.

They may also be afraid of your reaction. Households where communication only happens over the dinner table are spaces where secrets are the most common. The lack of communication and support from the parents teaches the child to stay quiet, because they have either been scolded when they come clean about something, had to give up their gadgets, or were grounded for it. None of these prospects are appealing to a teenager, so they keep quiet.

And finally, there is disapproval and disappointment that kids don't want their parents to feel towards them. So, they change their grades from a 'D' to an 'A' on their report card.

Things My Child Doesn't Want Me to Know

Now that we understand the motivations behind secrecy, it is time to note the many lies or secrets they will tell or keep from you whether you believe it or not. Some people who tend to be rather open and communicative with their kids are shocked when they find out that their children have been hiding things from them. It is only a matter of time before you find lingerie you didn't buy them or a packet of cigarettes in their coat.

Here's what they will hide from you 90% of the time.

They Are Friends With People You Don't Approve Of

As parents, it isn't hard for us to spot which friends are keepers and which aren't. Call it a sixth sense, but we get a bad feeling about some of their friends. But hcrc's the thing: despite you telling your kid to stay away from them for their own good, they are going to stay friends with them. They may not meet in the open like before, but they will stay in touch.

They Are on Social Platforms You Can't Track

Platforms like Facebook and Twitter are for old people now as there isn't much secrecy left, so kids are getting smarter in their choices of social media to keep their secrecy. They are signing up on platforms that keep their identity hidden or that are too complicated to be understood by a parent. You can never fully know what they are up to online.

They Are or Trying to Be Sexually Active

We have all lived through puberty when hormones start doing their thing. If your child, who is in their teens, isn't sexually active, they are trying to be. It is best to have the dreaded talk about protection and being safe sooner rather than later.

They Are Lying About Sleepovers

Have their sleepovers increased in the past few months? Do you always feel like they overdress a little to go to a sleepover? Chances are they are sneaking off to places they don't want you to find out about because you won't approve of them. This is a common secret among teenagers. They are always looking for excuses to party and be in places they aren't supposed to be in.

What Secrets Are Okay to Keep and What Aren't?

Keeping in mind the many secrets they may have been keeping from you, it is good to discuss what are good and bad secrets. Research suggests that kids often hide big secrets like assault or rape from their parents because they don't want to be viewed differently and they just want the thing to go away. However, as parents, it is our biggest fear that something bad will happen to our children and we won't be able to stop it. It is a proactive and sensible approach to know the difference between what secrets are acceptable and what aren't.

Secrets that are safe to keep

- Gossip about friends and family that are too petty to be disclosed in the open or that won't hurt them in some way.
- Surprised birthday parties organized for someone close to you as long as they don't violate someone's privacy.
- Information about gifts, which will be opened at a certain date or time and will no longer remain a secret then.
- Fun games as long as they are safe to play without supervision and don't involve harming someone's life.

Secrets that are unsafe to keep

- Being touched inappropriately, even if by a parent.
- Games that may harm someone or ruin their life.
- Photos or videos of someone that would otherwise be considered obscene or pornographic.
- The request for favors from someone that aren't appropriate in exchange for a gift or favor.
- Gossip about someone's sexuality or life that would ruin their reputation.
- Anything that bothers you enough that you can't get your head around it.

Chapter 5: What Am I Doing Wrong?

Now that we are aware of their motives and the things they keep from us, it is best to develop and establish an understanding with the children to involve you in their plans and share with you more. They must, at all times, know that they can come to you with their problems and worries. When they know that they will be listened to and valued, they will feel more comfortable sharing and opening up.

However, when parents try to do this, they often cross the line between being supportive and become invasive. Instead of becoming active listeners, they try to 'fix' the issues for them. The emphasis should be on trying to hear them, rather than problem-solve for them. Once we learn the difference between the two, it will be much easier to communicate without reacting to the things they tell you.

To better highlight the mistakes you might be making, below are some things you need to take note of and try your best not to resort to them.

Mistakes Parents Make When Struggling to Prevent Secrecy

For starters, they themselves teach kids to keep secrets. When was the last time you told your child to keep a secret for you? Was it when you two baked a cake for daddy on his birthday and didn't tell him until he got back home? Were you not the one to encourage them to lie for you when they talked to their dad on the phone? The more frequently you expect your children to lie on your behalf or share only half-truths, the more they will see it as a good thing. It is okay to have a few secrets every now and then don't make it a habit. As a parent, the first mistake you make is teaching your children to lie for you. Other than that:

Expecting Them to Keep Secrets

Kids are naïve and forgetful. You may have told them to keep a secret but even you know they are quick to open their mouth and let it all out. So, to add an extra layer of protection over your secret, you bribe them to stay true to their end of the bargain. "If you don't tell this to anyone, I will take you to the mall tomorrow and you can get a toy."

And there is the second mistake. You gave them a strong motive to keep their mouth shut, which is also telling them that if someone offers something of value in return, it is best to keep quiet. The reason this mistake is so serious is that groomers and pedophiles use these tactics when preying on children. They tell them to stay quiet about what goes on between them in exchange for a bag of chocolates or candies. Now, since you have been doing the same with your child i.e. bribing them with goods and things of their interest, they assume this is how things work and stay quiet. You can imagine the rest yourself.

Being Dishonest

Another mistake parents make is giving kids their impression that lying is an acceptable trait. If they see you lying, they will think that it is okay to hide things or lie about them because mommy and daddy do it too. So, the next time you make up an excuse about having a headache and skipping work or lying on the phone to some friend, make sure your child isn't in the same room as you. Of course, you may have your reasons to lie, but don't do it in front of the kids.

Not Speaking of the Dangers of Lying

Every parent has to sit down with their children and talk about the dangers of secrecy and lying. If you haven't done that already and they are still unable to make the connection between good and bad lies, then you are at fault here, not them. So, the next time they hide stuff, it's on you, not them!

Not Talking About the Repercussions of Lying

Sadly, not many parents recognize the repercussions secrecy can have. We have all seen TV shows and movies where teenagers hide rape and assault they witnessed but kept quiet to save themselves from being expelled or getting grounded by their parents. There have been cases where children lied to their parents to go to a party and ended up drunk-driving and injuring pedestrians. Not telling your children about how grave the consequence of secrecy can be is a serious mistake that could end up putting them in danger.

Refusing to Punish the Child Over Lying

If your children have been caught sneaking and hiding things from you, not punishing them for it gives them the impression that is okay to lie and keep secrets. How else will they get over a bad habit if you continue to act normal about it? They must be disciplined, if not punished, to prevent them from keeping secrets in the future.

Effective Ways to Prevent Secrecy

Now that we are aware of the dangers of secrecy and the mistakes many parents unintentionally make, how do we put an end to it? How do we teach our kids to stop keeping secrets and nip the habit in the bud? Here are a few workable strategies to apply.

Teach Them About Safe and Unsafe Secrets

The first step to preventing secrecy and encouraging transparency is teaching your children the difference between the two so that they are clearly aware of what is good and acceptable and what is bad and unacceptable. When they are able to make the distinction, they will less likely to be quiet about unsafe or bad secrets.

Discuss Daily Routines and Activities

Find a suitable time to have a detailed chat about how their day went, what they did, and who they engaged with. Ask them about their friends and teachers and how they feel about them. Inquire if they are happy at school and not hiding something unsafe or bad from you. Be calm while doing so or else the child will feel like you are violating their privacy.

Win Their Trust

All kids, big or small, crave space. The best way to provide them with it and still be sure nothing suspicious goes on without your knowledge is by gaining their trust and confidence. If they come to you to gossip about someone and tell you strictly to not share it with anyone as it is confidential, then value that! Don't go behind their back telling the whole world about it, because when they find out, they will no longer trust you.

Be an Active Listener

Sometimes, kids just want to be heard by someone so that they can voice their concerns and worries. When your child comes to you with confidence that you will offer some advice, use that time to talk to them, rather than disciplining or lecturing them, especially when they have made a mistake and are feeling guilty about it. This is the time to let them know that they have your undying support and to encourage them to come up with a way to rectify the situation.

Chapter 6: Encouraging Openness

Ever seen a caterpillar going through the various stages of metamorphosis to grow into a beautiful butterfly? Kids grow up in the same manner. With good values, high morals, and effective, healthy communication binding the whole family together, they become the best versions of themselves.

But the transition isn't sudden. There are many challenges along the way, mental and physical barriers that endanger the process of becoming independent, emotionally intelligent, and confident.

It is no secret that healthy relationships are only possible when healthy communication prevails. There are instances where the parent-child relationship suffers because of poor communication or misunderstandings. To prevent distance and rift in relationships, it is important that parents ensure openness towards the ideas and thoughts of their children so that they don't leave anything out when confiding in you.

In this chapter, we will discuss the role of family conversations and how they can minimize the habit of lying and secrecy in kids.

Importance of Healthy Communication

Spoken communication is the essence of the relationship between you and your child. It is highly unlikely that kids brought up in households where communication isn't valued or happens infrequently will grow up to become strong, confident, and self-reliant individuals. They go on to lead lives lacking love and compassion and have a hard time building meaningful relationships with their partners and friends.

Conversely, when communication is common and happens every day, children learn about the world and how it works from the experience of their parents. They are able to be expressive, open up, and share their thoughts and feelings without ever feeling awkward.

But can it also prevent lying and secrecy?

If you are looking for a short answer then YES, IT CAN!

If we go back and look at the reasons for lying and secret-keeping, we notice that both of them arise from a form of fear. The children fear being punished or causing disappointment. They are afraid that if they come clean, they will be punished. This leads to secrecy or telling half-truths. Effective communication between the parent and the child forges an environment where things are discussed no matter how absurd their nature. Things are shared without judgment and sensible ways to right the wrong or prevent the same mistakes are advised. When kids feel heard and have their opinions valued, there is nothing left for them to hide. It relieves them to have someone who is there to listen and help them with their problems. Additionally, it boasts a child's confidence and self-esteem when they know they can rely on someone completely. They feel more empowered and backed by the connection they have with you.

Effective Ways to Improve Parent-Child Communication

Sadly, there aren't any parental manuals that teach parents what to do and what not to do. As each child is unique and beautiful in their own way, so is the style of raising them. There are up to six different types of parenting styles, which suggest that there is no universal method to guarantee to raise successful and happy kids. But since it all starts with how good or bad the communication between the child and the parent is, we first need to ensure that we are doing all in our power to strengthen our bond with them so that they can learn to trust us and rely on us to help them get past hardships and obstacles.

Be an Interested Parent

Who is a parent? Is he/she only a meal provider, a diaper-changer, or a sleeping cushion? No, a parent is much more than that. A parent listens to their child with genuine concern and curiosity. A parent, at times, goes overboard with emotions like standing to applaud for them when overwhelmed with their performance on stage. They are the listening ear kids need, the comfort they turn to when sick, tired, or scared.

Don't Argue Over "Who is Right"

To establish healthy communication where the child continues to look up to you for support, approval, and correction is pivotal. Often, parents, being more experienced and cultured, try to argue with children over who's right. Clearly, you must be but they are too naïve to see that. No one likes to be told that they are wrong, even when they are wrong. Turning every conversation into a fight about who's wrong and who's right, isn't going to help you. Instead, it will further distance you from your child and promote the habit of lying and secrecy. Keep your cool and listen attentively without judgment. Let them have their say and then, if asked, offer solutions and advice.

Include Them in Decision-Making

Another way to pave the way for healthy communication is by seeking their opinion over family matters that will affect them too. For instance, you and your partner may have decided to take a trip to Greece and you tell your kid that you are going to go there this summer. You thought they would be over the moon with the news, but they seem heartbroken. Upon inquiring, you find out that they wanted to go to Disneyland all this time and had been waiting to talk to you about it over the weekend. If they don't feel that their voice matters and opinions are valued, they will stop putting them forward.

Ask Them About Their Needs

Many kids aren't expressive when it comes to talking about their needs. They feel pushy and demanding and thus, find means to get things by themselves. As a parent, talk to them about their needs often. Maybe, what they need isn't something materialistic but rather help to solve a problem or advice to overcome hardship. Or maybe they just want to vent their frustration with someone to unburden themselves a little.

Avoid Imposing Ideas

If your child is opening up to you, it means that they genuinely feel that you can offer opinions and support. However, if you continue to impose your ideas over how they should do things instead of giving them the power to choose, it will drive them away. Parents who respond with close-minded opinions and act uptight do more harm than good. Instead of imposing things, try to have a dialogue with your children, where both of you share your ideas and opinions and then choose the one that seems the best. Moreover, stop trying to control them or problem-solve for them as it makes them feel trapped.

Chapter 7: Act like a Role Model - Period!

Nearly all of the habits our children pick up are the ones they see us embodying. Some are of course genetic like sleeping in the same pose as their father or making noises while chewing like their mother. However, all the other habits and behaviors are considered a skill which means that can be learned upon repetition. As a parent, you have to be extra careful about what behaviors your children are picking up from you when you are not noticing. They have been looking up to you for nearly everything since birth. In this chapter, we briefly go over the role of parents as ideal models for their kids and discuss the positive habits that will help parents raise transparent and honest kids.

Dear Parents, It all Starts with You

Youngsters mostly look up to or want to establish relationships with people older and wiser than themselves. They find mentors in their teachers, relatives, or parents. However, not everyone becomes a role model for them. They may love their parents but not consider them role models. They may be fascinated by someone for a different set of skills. For instance, if they are into the piano or violin, they may consider a professional player as their role model because they want to be just like them. An ideal role model must possess some desirable traits which are easy to follow and look up to. They must ignite passion and inspire motivation to change in the follower. They must help them thrive towards their goals and push them forward with their personal story, determination, or personality.

If you want to become your child's role model, here are the qualities you must demonstrate.

- **Role Models Have Good Morals and Values**

  Good values and morals rank the highest. Any role model must be able to inspire others with the work that they do and how they do it. Children only respect people who stay true to their words and practice what they preach. They are people who support the right causes and raise their voice against violence and rights violations. They are also honest and far from deceit.

- **Role Models Practice Acceptance**

  They don't disregard others or think of others beneath them. They have the drive to help others in their community and area of work. They want others to improve and be better human beings. They don't take pleasure in belittling someone. They are someone who, upon seeing someone in need, goes to their aid no matter what their circumstances or background is.

- **Role Models Overcome Obstacles Fearlessly**

Unlike others, role models don't fear hardship but rather welcome it. They don't measure their success by where they are in their lives but rather by how many obstacles they have faced and overcome in their lives. Young people want to feel this empowered too. So this quality of braveness and commitment to not give up really speaks to them.

- **They are Creative and Optimistic**

According to a youngster, a role model is someone that detests monotony. They have a positive outlook on life and are usually upbeat and happy. They are people who see the good in everything and the bright side of things even when situations are bad. They are always looking at creative means to improve their current state and do something that helps them and others in their surroundings.

- **They Have Clear-cut Values**

Kids admire people who are able to live the life they visualize. They rely strongly on good and positive values. They never bend their morals to meet the requirements of someone else. They are always advocating for innovation and social change. The reason kids and teenagers admire thes traits is because someday they want to feel the same way and having someone like that in their life just makes the task seem less daunting.

- **Role Models Respect Others**

    Being respectful is another important trait of a role model. Not only do they value the people around them, but they also have respect for them. Like adults, kids want to feel respected too. They want their opinions to be valued and respected. They appreciate anyone that does so. According to them, role models should be selfless and hold non-prejudiced views.

4 Things Parents Who Raise Honest Kids do

Now that we have identified the mistakes and taken note of the things we do wrong, whether it is our timing or the way we are trying to communicate with our children, we now know what needs changing in order to raise honest kids. Remember when we were kids: we would spend hours playing with friends from the neighborhood, and there was always that one friend who was so chill about the scary ideas we sometimes had, like going to that empty house at the corner of the street or riding bikes without our hands on the handle? These were the sort of things we kept from our parents but not them. They would gloat about the activities of the day without fearing their reaction and response: their parents also seemed so interested and less judgmental than ours.

If you are still in touch with that friend, try to notice how different they are from you, who hid things from your parents, and lied about the days' activities. Notice the difference in the sort of relationship they have with everyone around them, especially their kids. Doesn't it feel like they have it all figured out and raising honest, confident, and independent kids?

The values and morals we model in ourselves are the ones our offspring take from us. It's like it rubs off them. This is why we must, at all times, be teaching them the habits that will help them improve their chances in the future, whether in terms of interpersonal relationships, career, or in life.

So, take a look at these four things that parents who raise honest kids have in them and try to embody the same in yourself.

1. They Model Honesty

Teaching kids the difference between right and wrong, good and bad, and acceptable and unacceptable behaviors and actions early on is an essential step to raising honest kids. Parents who understand this don't lie in front of their children. They speak the truth, even about the small things they could have easily lied about. For example, your mom came to pick you up from school while your dad waited at home. Your mother notices a friend of hers on the sidewalk and stops to have a chat. When you guys return and your father asks what took you so long, your mother doesn't answer with lies like 'getting stuck in traffic' but rather speaks the truth.

2. They Accept Their Mistakes

We are all humans and thus, prone to making mistakes. Parents make mistakes too but rather than hiding them, they accept them to teach their children that this is what they should do too. Owning up to one's mistakes takes courage. Seeing their parents own up to their mistakes without guilt or shame teaches c children to do the same too.

3. They're Authoritative

They are controlling but not dictators. They allow their kids to make mistakes so that they can learn valuable lessons about honesty and the dangers of secrecy that can only be learned with experience. They don't punish their children because they know that only promotes a culture of secrecy and lying. Instead, they discipline them in a calm manner. That doesn't mean there are no consequences for the way they behave, it is just that they aren't harsh or brutal.

4. They Wait before Judging

No one has ever learned a new skill in a day. If we want to learn a new language, it takes classes and extensive coaching to be able to speak it fluently. It's the same with habits. The more we practice them, the better we get at them. This is what parents try to raise honest kids to understand. They know that learning to speak the truth and not keep secrets takes time. Children need to feel confident that they can go to their parents and discuss anything and everything. They need to first develop an understanding with their parents, and the parents needs to allow them as much time as they need. They don't rush them to act well-mannered in a day and lose all bad habits. They allow their children to gradually make the transition on their own terms.

Chapter 8: Raising an Honest Child

Raising an honest child is hard. There will be times you will find yourself lying to their face about something the minute you are teaching them not to lie. Not to mention, they will be least bothered by the upcoming lecture because one, according to them they don't lie and two, they are still going to at least continue with the hiding part because that is an essential part of growth.

So that leaves you with fewer chances of success, especially if they are already in their teens and looking at you as a potential enemy, someone rather uptight and backward.

However, if you approach the topic in ways that don't come off as lecturing but rather healthy discussions in the form of storytelling, you may increase your chances of getting them thinking. This will be the first step towards victory.

In this final chapter of the book, we will list ways that will help you get your voice heard loud and clear. Practice these and later pat yourself on the back for having raised an honest child.

Responding to Lies – Strategies to Help Parents Improve Transparency

Honesty a habit that never loses its charm and continues to add to one's respect and reputation. So how do we raise honest children, you ask? Here's how:

Model Honesty

This goes without saying and seems rather obvious too, but kids observe and they imitate. If you aren't being the perfect flag-bearer for honesty, they aren't going to hear a word of it. If you lie to your kids, whether it is for their safety or out of worry, they will see it as a means to get away with things. When kids see their parents preaching about honesty on one hand and telling lies on the other, it sends them mixed signals which they are too young to comprehend. If they are too young to make the distinction between safe and unsafe, and acceptable and unacceptable lies, they will have a hard time listening to you and modeling honesty within themselves.

Don't Provide Them with Opportunities to Lie

Don't invite lying. One way parents bring it onto themselves is by providing the child with opportunities to lie as a way of testing them. If you notice they have spilled a glass of juice on their shirts or used your lipstick, don't ask them who did it or how it happened. 99% of the time, after being caught red-handed, children are going to lie and blame someone else. You already know who did what, so instead of offering them a chance to lie, simply say, "Looks like you have spilled some juice, let's go clean it up and be careful the next time" or "I see you have used mommy's lipsticks without her permission. Let's get you cleaned up and please ask permission to use it next time."

Notice how these sentences eliminate or lessen the burden of blame and make the conversation less confrontational? Chances are, if they paid attention and realized that not every mistake is rewarded with punishment and shame, they will try to come to clean next time.

Teach Them to Say the Hard Truths

Sometimes, it is more important to uphold morals than to care about someone getting hurt. For example, your son's friend has a habit of stealing things whenever they visit your house. Your son might have known and kept a secret, assuming you won't find out. However, as a responsible parent, it is your job to encourage your son to do the right thing and tell his friend to stop stealing. Of course, the friend will deny any attempt at stealing first and will have their feelings hurt, but it will also set them on the right path if they choose to quit.

Stop Rewarding Lies

When a child lies, there is usually something motivating them. There is a reason why they decide to hide the truth, and if you reward them with what they are seeking, they begin to see it as an effective strategy. Stop giving them what they need until they tell you why they need it. Don't reward their every wish and demand without realizing that it will eventually spoil them and make them feel privileged.

Praise Them When Honest

On the other hand, if you do want to reward them, reward them when you see them telling the truth. Catch them telling the truth, act elated that they did, and reward this behavior with an ice-cream treat or more time watching TV. The point is, when they notice a certain behavior leads to a prize, they will try to model more of it – just for the sake of the reward.

Keep Promises

If they keep finding you breaking your promises to them, they will do the same. Thus, it is again down to becoming the role model they would want to follow. Keep promises to ensure the trust between you and your children isn't broken.

Be Calm While Disciplining

A lot of times, we respond to a lying act rather harshly. We yell and punish the child for lying and take away their gadgets, or ground them at home. In households where punishments are doled out harshly, kids learn to lie earlier. This doesn't mean there isn't any need to discipline them, but rather it means it's best to impart discipline in a calm and composed manner. If they have been caught lying or have come to you to tell the truth, don't have an emotional reaction. Simply state the facts as to why they shouldn't have lied and should try not to, moving forward.

Mess Up Some Facts

One of the most fun ways of teaching them about honesty is by messing up some common facts in the stories or poems they love. For example, Mary had a little 'cat' instead of a 'lamb'. Let them point out the messed up fact. You can also make false statements like you are wearing a red-colored shirt when in reality, it is yellow. When children feel challenged in such a manner, they learn about the impact of a lie and how it can change the whole story.

Set Clear Expectations

Another important thing parents must do is be clear about what is expected of them. They must know the rules they must abide by to avoid disappointment and lying. Kids tend to lie when the expectations are either too high or hazy and they don't end up living up to them. So to avoid embarrassment and shaming, they lie to get away.

Give Them Privacy

It doesn't matter how young or old they are, privacy and space is an essential thing to offer your children. Being overprotective or adopting a 'helicopter parenting' style would only make them feel suffocated, which will lead them to start making excuses and tell lies to get you off their back. Don't be too intrusive and wait for them to come to you if something is bothering them.

Share Positive Stories

If they are still young, it is the best time to read stories about characters who lied but came clean about their mistake or wrongdoing to their parents. According to a research study led by psychologist Kang Lee at the University of Toronto, children aged three to seven are more likely to be inspired by positive stories than negative ones. This means that stories that end up scaring them at the end like the *Boy who Cried Wolf* aren't going to be as impactful as *George Washington and the Cherry Tree*.

Make Promise to Them

If you are curious about something they did or something that happened to them, before asking them to tell you all about it, ask them to promise you first that they will answer only with the truth when you ask a question. This increases the likelihood of them speaking the truth. However, this should be used rarely, or else it will lose its efficacy.

Conclusion

Being a parent, in its essence, is a demanding role. Even though we sign up for it willingly and cheerfully, we mustn't forget the challenges it brings along with it. As your baby grows into a toddler, child, adolescent, and into a teenager, their needs grow too. They no longer rely on you for feeds, sleep, and cleaning only. To make a respectable place for themselves in the world out there, they also need good morals, ethics, and values to live by.

Teaching them to be honest and respectable are the core values we instill in them and yet, despite our best efforts, we often catch them lying straight to our faces with confident-eyes and a calm tone. So where are we doing wrong? Why do they still turn to lie, deceit, and secrecy when we teach them not to? This is rather complicated and also the goal of the book. Not only did we want to give parents the answer to this, but we also wanted them to explore with us the many things that they are doing wrong. Things, like being dishonest themselves, keeping secrets, and teaching their children to keep secrets for them, are few of the mistakes we make.

But there is a light at the end of the tunnel. We now have the means to prevent secrecy and model honesty in our children using tools like open and supportive communication, becoming an ideal role model to them, and teaching them about the dangers of secrecy and lying.

With continued work, the right values will make a home in their hearts and help you, as a parent, to take some pressure off your shoulders. Once they learn of the many advantages being honest and transparent has, they will, themselves, choose to respect others and value their feelings.

Thank you for giving this book a read. I hope you loved reading it as much as I enjoyed writing it. It would make me the happiest person on earth if you would take a moment to leave an honest review. All you have to do is visit the site where you purchased this book: It's that simple! The review doesn't have to be a full-fledged paragraph; a few words will do. Your few words will help others decide if this is what they should be reading as well. Thank you in advance, and best of luck with your parenting adventures. Every moment is a joyous one with a child.

References

5 Types of Liars and How to Spot Them. (2019, October 8). https://www.womenworking.com/5-types-of-liars-and-how-to-spot-them/

Francis, L. (2020, February 26). Honest Kids Come From Parents Who Do These 5 Things. https://www.fatherly.com/parenting/parents-honest-kids-5-things/

Feldman, R. (2002, June 10). UMass researcher finds most people lie in everyday conversation. Hampshire County, Massachusetts, United States.

Heid, M. (n.d.). Your Brain On: Lying. https://www.shape.com/lifestyle/mind-and-body/your-brain-lying

Honesty Really Is Healthy. (2012, August 8). https://www.huffpost.com/entry/honesty-healthy-lies-truth_n_1748144

How to Prevent Kids from Keeping Secrets. (n.d.). https://www.indiaparenting.com/raising-children/130_5389/how-to-prevent-kids-from-keeping-secrets.html

It's A Thin Between Privacy & Secrecy. (2018, February 5). https://couplesacademy.org/2018/02/05/its-a-thin-between-privacy-secrecy/

Kelly, A. E. (2012, August 4). Lying Less Linked to Better Health, New Research Finds. Orlando, Florida, United States of America.

Levine, E. E., & Cohen, T. R. (2018). You can handle the truth: Mispredicting the consequences of honest communication. Journal of Experimental Psychology: General, 1400–1429.

Ni, P. (2015, July 22). 7 Key Signs of a Lying Child or Teenager. https://www.psychologytoday.com/us/blog/communication-success/201507/7-key-signs-lying-child-or-teenager

Pssst...Why Is My Teen Keeping Secrets From Me? (2011, July 31). https://www.psychologytoday.com/us/blog/youth-and-tell/201107/pssstwhy-is-my-teen-keeping-secrets-me

Smith, C. E., & Rizzo, M. T. (2017). Children's confession- and lying-related emotion expectancies: Developmental differences and connections to parent-reported confession behavior. Journal of Experimental Child Psychology, 113-128.

Smith, J. A. (n.d.). What's Good about Lying? https://greatergood.berkeley.edu/article/item/whats_good_about_lying

The Secret Lives of Teens They Don't Want You to
Know About. (2019, May 20).
https://www.allprodad.com/the-secret-lives-
of-teens-they-dont-want-you-to-know-about/

Why Honesty Is Good for Our Kids' Health. (2020,
April 20). https://www.parent.com/honesty-
good-kids-health/

Verschuere, B., Spruyt, A., Meijer, E. H., & Otgaar, H.
(2010). The ease of lying. Consciousness and
Cognition, 908-11.